UNDERSTANDING AND PREVENTING

D0815336

TEEN SUICIDE

**Written and photographed by
Warren Colman**

*HV
6546
.C65
1990*

 CHILDRENS PRESS ®
CHICAGO

All names of persons in this book who have been involved in a suicide episode or attempt have been changed to protect individual privacy. Any similarity in names of persons in this bok and actual individuals is coincidental. All photographs in this book are re-enactments and persons in them are shown for illustrative purposes only.

Library of Congress Cataloging-in-Publication Data

Colman, Warren.
    Understanding and preventing teen suicide / written & photographed by Warren Colman.
        p.   cm.
    Summary: Discusses possible causes of teenage suicide, the effects on the family, and ways to prevent the suicide of friends.
    ISBN 0-516-00594-4
    1. Teenagers—United States—Suicidal behavior—Juvenile literature.   2. Suicide—United States—Prevention—Juvenile literature.   [1. Suicide.]   I. Title.
    HV6546.C65   1990
    362.2'8'0835—dc20   90-1400
                                                                      CIP
                                                                      AC

Cover and interior designed by Sara Shelton.

Copyright © 1990 by Childrens Press®, Inc.
Printed in the United States of America.
1 2 3 4 5 6 7 8 9 10 R 98 97 96 95 94 93 92 91 90

UNDERSTANDING AND PREVENTING

TEEN SUICIDE

C O N T E N T S

v

The teen years can be a time for having fun and expanding hori-zons. But the enormous stresses caused by the physical and emotional changes of adolescence can result in problems that may seem overwhelming.

CHAPTER 1

The Life and Death
of Melissa K.

To all outward appearances, Melissa K.'s life seemed perfect. She lived in a Tudor mansion set on a large wooded lot. The house had its own private beach on Lake Michigan.

Melissa's home was once featured in a national architectural magazine. A photograph of her bedroom spread across two pages showed Melissa on a large window seat, reading a book. Behind her, through the semicircular window, exquisite fall foliage was punctuated by a deep blue sky and sparkling water. Towering golden oaks outside the window, slightly out of focus, formed a halo around Melissa's silhouette. The photographer said it was one of the most beautiful pictures he had ever taken.

On summer weekends, Melissa and her friends played volleyball on the beach behind her house. The cook would fix lunches and dinners for everyone, and the maid would bring the food to the shore.

Melissa, nicknamed Cookie by her family and friends, was a model student, smart enough to be in several honors classes. And she was a hard worker, a dedicated student who frequently did extra-credit assignments to maintain her 3.6 average.

Whenever Cookie's mother felt depressed, she would take her daughter shopping. The two would spend the afternoon exploring fashionable boutiques nestled along Sheridan Road, on Chicago's exclusive North Shore. Mrs. K. said her daughter's sunny disposition would, in her words, "wash away the depression."

Cookie's friends felt the same way. She always had time to listen to their problems. Cookie seldom, if ever, discussed her own. She was immensely popular at school, the kind of girl whose bubbly personality attracts others—both boys and girls.

In the spring of 1988, however, Cookie changed. For reasons no one can explain, she became withdrawn. When her friends asked her to go to the movies or to a party, she told them she had other plans. She spent more and more time alone in her room. She refused to go shopping with her mother.

In the fall, Melissa's parents flew to Frankfurt, West Germany, where Dr. K., an executive for a large pharmaceutical company, was scheduled to speak at an international conference.

Cookie's grandmother was looking after her and

her two brothers in their parents' absence. Mrs. K. was worried about Cookie, but convinced herself that her daughter was "just going through a phase."

At 2:24 in the morning, three days after their arrival in Frankfurt, the phone rang in Dr. and Mrs. K.'s hotel suite. Dr. K.'s brother was on the line. Choking back tears, he said that Melissa had been found in the woods near their home. She had hanged herself.

Melissa K. committed suicide thirty-seven days before her sixteenth birthday. Her seemingly perfect life ended, and she became another grim statistic in a growing national tragedy.

During the past quarter century, the suicide rate has tripled among young people fifteen to twenty-four years old. More than five thousand teens now take their own lives each year in the United States.

According to the National Center for Health Statistics, teen suicides have increased nearly fourfold since 1960.

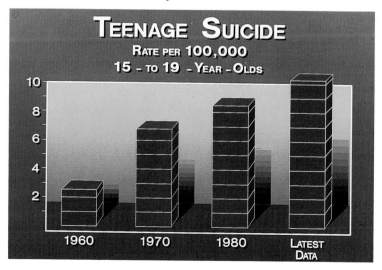

TEENAGE SUICIDE
RATE PER 100,000
15 - TO 19 - YEAR - OLDS

Equally troubling, about half a million teenagers attempt suicide annually.

Officially, suicide is the third largest cause of death among teens in the United States, ranking behind only accidents and murders.

But some mental health authorities believe that the official statistics don't tell the real story; they maintain that suicide may really be the number two killer of young people.

These experts say that many deaths are inaccurately reported as accidents. They contend that officials sometimes classify a suicide as an accident in order to spare the feelings of the victim's family. Other times, they say, a suicide *appears* to be an accident—and is reported as such. Many fatal auto crashes are believed to fall into this category.

Teens killing themselves, then, is a sad reality in modern America—a reality that all of us would do well to understand. For only through understanding will we be able to confront this tragedy and conquer it.

Ignoring teen suicide, according to the experts, is an almost certain way for more lives to be lost.

This book is an attempt to help you and other young people understand the problem and its possible causes. It is also an attempt to show how you may help prevent a friend's needless death.

Perhaps above all else, the main lesson in the pages that follow is this: No matter how sad and bleak one's

According to many experts, teens who are killed in automobile wrecks are sometimes incorrectly classified as accident victims. In reality, the teen has attempted suicide by driving recklessly.

life may appear to be—and it can be very sad and bleak indeed—there are *always* better ways than suicide to deal with despair.

Many teens feel insecure and awkward when starting a relationship with a member of the opposite sex.

CHAPTER 2

The Teen Years: Tough Times

Perhaps no teenager has ever been able to sail through the stormy seas of adolescence free from emotional pain. It's just not in the cards. Simply put, the teen years are a time of enormous physical and emotional change.

And almost all changes produce stress. That's because a person undergoing changes is often unsure of how those changes will affect his or her life.

One of the most important changes in adolescence is the physical attraction boys and girls begin to feel for each other. But, being new at the boy-likes-girl/girl-likes-boy game, neither knows very much about the rules. Knowing how to act in the presence of members of the opposite sex when there's a mutual attraction is like anything else. It takes time to become an expert.

So those first attempts at getting to know the opposite sex are usually very awkward.

And when people are awkward, they feel inferior. (Feeling inferior is an occupational hazard for a teen.) Unfortunately, those feelings of inadequacy can be extremely intense.

The desire for independence is something else that conspires against emotional stability during the teen years. As youngsters spread their wings and venture beyond the direct influence of their parents, conflicts often arise.

Friction between parents and teens may occur when youngsters attempt to assert their independence.

Friction between parents and their teenage children takes many different forms, of course. For the most part, however, it centers on youngsters wanting to be their own persons, free from parental control.

Strife between teens and parents is nothing new. Ancient writings discovered by archaeologists in Iraq tell about a father who, five thousand years ago, scolded his son for being lazy. When the son protested, the father said, "You and your friends hang around the city square, doing nothing all day. And you show no respect toward your elders."

Sound familiar?

Tom S. could probably relate to that Iraqi youth.

When Tom's freshman basketball team, the Chiefs, reached the district semifinals, he and his fellow players decided to get Mohawk haircuts to display team solidarity. A few parents shrugged; most of the others protested in varying degrees. Tom's father, however, was adamant. "No son of mine is ever going to get one of those freak haircuts," he insisted.

Pointing his finger at Tom, he added emphatically, "If you ever show up with that strip on your head, you'll be grounded until the rest of your hair grows back. And that means no tournament!"

Furious at his father, Tom stalked to his room and slammed the door.

Hairstyles, clothing, makeup, curfews, grades, allowances, leisure-time activities—all offer an opportunity for conflict between teens and parents.

Friendships provide emotional support for teens.

Along with becoming increasingly independent, and establishing a sexual identity, having conflicts with parents is tough for any teenager to handle.

But there's another, less obvious factor in such conflicts.

When teens begin to lose their strong ties to their parents, they need to find a replacement. Not an *exact* replacement, but someone or something to help ensure that they won't be alone.

So teenagers turn to their friends. They form cliques. (Tom's clique was the basketball team.) With their friends, they establish a sense of belonging. To teens who are emotionally breaking away from their

16

Being part of a group helps soften the emotional turmoil that may come when teens begin to break away from their parents.

parents, that sense of belonging can be the most important thing in the world.

That's because being alone is, for most people, one of life's most painful experiences. And for most teens, being alone is truly intolerable.

To prevent this feeling of isolation, many adolescents feel they must act like their friends.

Keeping that in mind, it's understandable why Tom was so angry at his father. The way Tom saw it, Mr. S. put him into a no-win situation: If he got a Mohawk, he wouldn't be allowed to help his teammates in the

Being alone can be truly intolerable for a teenager.

tournament. But if he didn't get a Mohawk, he would no longer be part of the group. He'd be an outsider. He'd be alone, the only one who didn't cut his hair for the team.

Of course, parents have a right—in fact, an obligation—to prevent their children from hurting themselves and others. Every parent, for example,

18

has the right to object to a child's using drugs. That's because drugs are dangerous, and everyone knows it. But some points of dispute, such as Mohawks, lie in a gray area. Not everybody would agree that a Mohawk is harmful.

After Tom went to his room, he had fleeting thoughts about how to get back at his father: He'd live at his best friend's house; he'd stay out all night; he'd get the Mohawk immediately before the game, play, then suffer the consequences of his father's wrath afterward.

But Tom did not consider killing himself. (To consider suicide over such a minor incident might seem preposterous to you. But as you'll see later, a suicidal person might not consider it preposterous at all.)

At this point, it's not important to understand why Tom was able to cope with the situation while another person might not. It's only important to understand that Tom, along with many other teens, *was* able to cope with the problems he faced—whether it was difficulties with parents, school, classmates, friends, or teachers.

It's also important to realize that every teen gets angry and depressed. There are too many things going on in an adolescent's life for it to be otherwise.

But it's equally important to know that over the past several decades, more and more teens have *not* been able to cope.

They have decided to kill themselves.

A stable family life is the most important ingredient in a child's emotional growth.

20

CHAPTER 3

Painful Changes in the American Family

No one knows for sure why teen suicide is on the rise. But many thoughtful scholars and mental health professionals have studied the subject. And they have come up with several possible reasons.

We all know that the teen years are difficult, and probably always have been. But being an adolescent in today's world is especially difficult. In fact, one scholar at Northwestern University has stated that, with the exception of the Middle Ages, life for teenagers is more difficult today than in any other period of history.

Of course, that doesn't mean that young people suffer unrelenting mental torture every hour of every day. If you're about to enter your teen years, there are lots of wonderful things to eagerly anticipate.

For the first time, you'll probably fall deeply in

Expanding horizons with a hobby such as music or computers is one of the best things about being a teenager.

love. And that can be terrific. Flexing newfound physical abilities is also a great experience. And expanding your mind through a hobby such as computers, chess, art, or literature can be an equally satisfying experience.

Doing an increasing number of things on your own generates a wonderful sense of achievement. And developing deep, abiding friendships that will last a lifetime is something that happens most often during the teen years. All these great things, and more, are yours for the taking.

But by now you know that life is far from perfect. You see trouble and tragedy every time you read a newspaper or watch a news program on television.

As wonderful as our country is, we've got some very serious problems. And many of those problems can directly affect your life as a teen.

Rootlessness is one of them. America, in many ways, has become a rootless society, a place where families move from one city to another many times.

Every time a family moves to a new location, it's hard on the children. It's especially hard on teens because their all-important friendships are lost or—at the very least—are difficult to maintain. And finding a new group of friends can be a frightening and stressful experience.

Moving had become especially hard on John F. John's father was an executive on a rapid climb up the corporate ladder. Every year or so, Mr. F. was promoted. With each promotion came a new job in another city. When John was very young, he found the moves upsetting. But at the end of each trek there would be a larger house and more toys.

As he got older, however, the novelty of bigger houses and larger rear-screen televisions began to wear thin. By the time he was sixteen, John had stopped trying to make friends in his new schools.

But several months after his latest move to a Denver suburb, he met Carla. She was his lab partner in chemistry class, and they hit it off immediately.

John simply couldn't help himself: he fell in love.

John and Carla dated steadily for six months. Then, one late spring evening, Mr. F. announced that the family would move to Atlanta in the summer.

After dinner, John went to the closet where his father kept a collection of hunting rifles and live ammunition. He took out one of the guns, loaded it, and pulled the trigger.

By the time the paramedics arrived, there was nothing that could be done.

In a note found next to his body, John wrote that he couldn't bear the pain of leaving Carla. For him, the move to Atlanta was one move too many.

Mr. and Mrs. F. did not understand how much strain all the moves had placed on their son. They had been born and reared in Kansas, and didn't leave their small town until they graduated from college. When they were children, their cousins, grandparents, aunts and uncles—their extended family—were no more than five or ten minutes away.

If either of them had a problem when their mother or father wasn't around, there was always a relative nearby who would listen sympathetically and perhaps give advice.

John didn't have an extended family nearby.

Mental health experts have known for a long time that the family is the most important factor in a child's emotional stability. In days past, members of the extended family could fill in if the parents weren't

When a parent moves out of the house, the child usually feels a deep sense of loss.

at home. Today, the extended family has become, for the most part, a thing of the past.

So, moving from place to place, and not having relatives nearby, are important parts of a story that could be called "Painful Changes in the American Family."

Divorce is another part of that story. Today, about one half of all marriages end up in divorce court. Even when a divorce is friendly, which is rare, children in the family usually have terrible feelings of guilt.

For although children seldom cause a divorce, they often *feel* that they do.

Youngsters often try to get their parents back together. And since that seldom happens, their feelings of guilt and frustration increase.

In addition, children of divorced couples almost always feel a deep sense of loss when a parent moves out of the house. And as you'll read in Chapter 12, that sense of loss can trigger a suicide attempt.

If there has been a lot of fighting before the divorce, the breakup may be viewed with a huge sigh of relief—even with eager anticipation.

But soon enough, it becomes clear that new problems have taken the place of the old ones.

When one parent leaves, many burdens fall on the shoulders of the other. Chores that were divided between Mom and Dad now must be done entirely by the remaining parent. Burdened by these tasks, the new single parent often has less time and energy to devote to the children.

To make matters worse, newly divorced mothers often must go back to work to ease the financial burdens that can come with a marriage breakup. Or they may take a second job. Children of divorced parents, then, may not spend much time with either parent.

But many youngsters desperately need that time, a daily period when a mother or father can help them overcome the terrible feelings that almost always come with divorce. And they need a parent around to reassure them that things eventually will get better.

Although divorce and rootlessness are major causes of the changes in the American family, there are still others. During the past quarter century, there has been a profound change in the role of women in

Many mothers now leave their children in day-care centers and then head off to work.

America. And that change, according to some experts, has been harmful to the family.

At one time, most women believed that their most important role was that of homemaker and mother. During the 1960s and 1970s, however, that view changed drastically. Some people in "the feminist movement" thought women were wasting their talents at home. They said women could better realize their potential in the workplace.

Many women left their children during the day and went to work. These children, unsupervised for part of the day, became known as "latchkey children." After school, latchkey children took the key from a shoelace around their neck, unlocked the door, and entered an empty house.

Communication between child and parent is important.

In the 1970s, some women felt they *had* to work outside the home. During that decade, the United States went through two economic recessions. The downturn that lasted from November 1973 to March 1975 was one of the worst recessions of the century.

To make matters worse, many Americans were forced to move from high-paying manufacturing jobs to lower-paying service jobs in the 1970s. Confronted with their husband's smaller paycheck, many women worked to help pay for the food, rent, and car loan.

Regardless of the reasons for women returning to work, there were no adults—and more important, no mother to talk to—when many children returned from school each day. An extremely important part of the family, a parent who could talk with the children, was missing during the afternoon hours.

Mental health experts stress the need for communication in families. Kids need to discuss problems

Many psychologists believe that *bonding* between mother and infant is needed for the child to feel good about himself or herself later in life.

and share triumphs with their parents. Parents need to explain rules of conduct. And they need to show pride in their youngsters' achievements, so that sons and daughters will feel good about themselves.

When mothers of very young children return to work soon after giving birth, something else of great importance, a process called *bonding,* may never take place. Many psychologists believe that bonding between infant and mother is an ingredient needed for the child to feel good about himself or herself in later life. Those who hold this view say that persons who have not bonded may be prone to suicide.

During the past several decades, then, parents have spent less and less time with their children. And, in most instances, there were no aunts, uncles, or grandparents nearby to take their place. So who has taken care of the children? The children themselves and the television set.

Many teenagers watch almost one thousand hours of television each year.

CHAPTER 4

The Media

According to many experts, television may be another culprit in the tragedy of teen suicide. No one can say with certainty the exact role television plays, but many authorities feel that it *is* a factor.

If you're like most other young people, you spend more time watching television than in any other activity. Statistics show that teenagers watch almost one thousand hours of TV programming each year.

Television programs can be entertaining and educational. But they can be terribly misleading, too, because they often present an unrealistic picture of life's problems. In addition—and equally disturbing to many people—TV shows often present an unrealistic view of how these problems are solved.

Characters in TV shows usually solve their problems in 22½ minutes. (Commercials take up the remaining 7½ minutes of each half-hour episode.) Of course, that makes for a neat, satisfying package of entertainment. But most certainly, it does *not* reflect real life, where serious personal problems may take years to develop, and also may take years to resolve.

Yet, to a young television viewer with only limited experience in the real world, the images on the screen may raise some very troubling questions: Why isn't *my* life so simple and enjoyable? Why can't *I* solve my problems in 22½ minutes?

The youngster may not even realize that he or she is asking those questions. They may lie deep inside the viewer's mind. Even so, those questions can build up a lot of frustration. And they point to a second problem—the young viewer's inability to tell the difference between fact and fiction.

Many mental health professionals say that kids who watch too much television often have a hard time separating fantasy from reality. And as you'll read later, this inability to separate fact from fiction can play a big role in suicide.

Something else that disturbs many authorities in the mental health field is the amount of violence on television. And experts find it equally disturbing that the violence is cleaned up, or "sanitized," so that viewers won't become too upset. Victims of TV violence don't bleed a lot, and seldom suffer very much—or for very long. This sanitized violence gives viewers a false impression of death and pain.

Movies and TV shows seldom reflect life as it really is.

Watching too much television may pose another hazard for teens because looking at a TV screen is such a passive activity. It's easy to just space out in front of the tube, letting your mind idle for hours on end.

But problems—personal or otherwise—cannot be solved passively. Solving personal problems *always* involves mental activity. Watching TV gives us no practice in using our minds actively to solve problems.

And so, according to some experts, when television addicts face a serious personal problem, they may not have developed the important mental tools needed to cope with it.

Solving personal problems almost always involves active communication, too. But people who sit hour after hour in front of the tube get no practice in the verbal give-and-take needed to communicate effectively. A person may talk back to people on a TV show or sing along with MTV, but that's *not* communicating.

There's no denying that rock video programs have become extremely popular in recent years. Most rock videos are very entertaining (the visual effects are often stunning) and generally harmless.

But according to a number of experts, a few rock tunes have prompted teen suicides. These authorities maintain that some songs contain lyrics that leave the very dangerous and erroneous impression that suicide is an acceptable way to deal with one's problems.

And *all* the experts agree that suicide is *not* an acceptable way. *All* the experts agree that there are much better ways to deal with life's problems.

Unfortunately, these authorities have had little apparent effect on groups such as Blue Oyster Cult, Loverboy, and Pet Shop Boys. All have performed songs that suggest suicide is justifiable when life becomes difficult.

One performer, Ozzy Osborne, released an album called *Blizzard of Oz* in the early 1980s. During one song on the album, Osborne sings, "Suicide is the only way out."

Some experts say that Ozzy Osborne, the rock star, has recorded songs that encourage teen suicide.

Another problem is that some rock stars—not many, but some—lead very glamorous, yet self-destructive lives. Lyrics that refer to the star's self-destructive behavior (usually that means taking drugs) can influence listeners. It's easy to get the impression that glamor and a self-destructive life-style go hand in hand. But, of course, they don't. A person can lead a glamorous life and not be self-destructive.

Finally, the way that news programs cover teen suicides has troubled many experts. Often, the coverage goes something like this:

> The reporter stands in front of a suburban house and solemnly says, "Cynthia P., a junior at Central High, took her own life today, leaving behind a community of shocked friends and puzzled neighbors."

The viewer now sees paramedics placing Cynthia's covered body in the ambulance. The report continues:

> "The quiet 17-year-old was discovered by her parents in the front seat of the family's station wagon, parked in a closed garage behind the family home on West Elm Street. The engine was still running at the time of the discovery."

Many experts have been troubled by the way the news media have covered teen suicides.

A group of neighbors watch as the ambulance pulls away:

> "Neighbors say they can't understand what prompted the tragedy."

Mr. Miller, the next-door neighbor, talks to the reporter:

> "Cynthia was our baby-sitter for the past three or four years. She was wonderful with our kids. She never seemed moody or anything like that. Why would she do it? It's beyond me. I can't figure it out."

Cynthia's best friend, who lives several streets away, now appears on the screen. She brushes tears aside as she speaks:

> "All I know is that every kid in school is going to be at the funeral. Everybody loved Cynthia. It's just so sad. Central won't be the same without her."

The reporter makes a few closing remarks, then throws it back to the reporters in the studio.

The entire story lasts about forty-five or fifty seconds. Like everything else in the fantasy world of television—even some of television news—it's clean, neat, and precise.

Cynthia's death has become a fifty-second event. The audience now knows that everybody loved Cynthia, she was a good baby-sitter, and that (maybe) a lot of kids will go to her funeral.

And to them, the funeral might just as well be another television show, the second episode of what might be called "Cynthia's Simple Suicide."

To many viewers, now watching a commercial break during which three animated bears sing the praises of a sugar-coated cereal, "Cynthia's Simple Suicide" doesn't seem quite so bad. After fifty seconds of mild discomfort, it's over.

For a more realistic look at suicide, stay tuned for the next chapter.

Dead people don't smell flowers, eat pizza, see a rainbow, or enjoy any of life's other pleasures.

CHAPTER 5

Fantasy vs. Reality

People who study suicides have known for a long time that most teens who try to kill themselves almost never have a full understanding of what they're about to do.

They simply don't grasp the true significance of death—that when a person is dead, he or she ceases to exist. A dead person can't hug a dog, smell a flower, look at a rainbow, hear a song, or taste a pepperoni pizza. And a dead person never will. A dead person never comes back. Never.

Like many other youngsters who attempt suicide, Michelle C. thought a great deal about how her friends and family would react to her death. Michelle's father was an alcoholic who had physically abused her since she was four years old. Her mother had abandoned the family when Michelle was ten, leaving the youngster to care for her two brothers, at that time aged nine and six.

For the past five years, Michelle had done the laundry and ironing, fixed the meals, washed the dishes, cleaned the house, done the shopping, gone to school, completed her homework, and tried to rear her brothers as best she could, with only occasional help from her widowed grandmother.

For her efforts, she received several beatings a week, whenever her father came home drunk.

After one particularly brutal beating, during which her nose was broken, Michelle began making specific plans for her death. Her scheme began to take shape in the emergency room of the hospital. As Michelle sat waiting to have her nose bandaged, she decided to swallow a bottle of her grandmother's sleeping pills.

The more she thought about it, the more the idea seemed to take on a life of its own. In her mind's eye, Michelle saw her own funeral. She saw her father weeping uncontrollably in the front row of the chapel. Overcome with remorse, he wailed, "It's all my fault! How could I have been so horrible to my own daughter?" Sadness would haunt him for the rest of his life.

"Good!" thought Michelle. "He deserves it!"

Michelle fantasized about *coming back* to see her father's grief. (Otherwise, how could she know for certain that he would be overcome with remorse?)

But if Michelle killed herself, she *wouldn't* come

Once people die, their bodies stay in the cemetery. Dead people never come back. Never.

back—despite anything she might have seen in the movies or on TV.

But let's suppose for a moment that Michelle *could* come back. And let's suppose that she *was* able to see her father's reaction to her death. And let's suppose he wasn't remorseful at all, or at least not as remorseful as Michelle thought he would be.

The end result? Michelle paid the ultimate price— her life—to get even. *And there was no payoff!*

Betting on "getting even" through a suicide is a no-win proposition. And so is killing oneself to escape one's problems.

Many youngsters who have attempted suicide, or who have seriously thought about it, report an enormous sense of relief once the decision to kill themselves has been made.

These teens often see themselves falling into a very long, restful sleep once they're no longer alive. In their new lifeless state, they think, they will exist peacefully in a never-never land where problems cease to exist. There, they finally will be free from pain—and will be happy. A wonderful thought.

But any number of examples show that these thoughts are nothing more than a sad delusion.

Michael L., a junior in high school, is just one example. Michael's parents were graduates of Princeton University, a prestigious Ivy League institution, and they wanted him to follow in their footsteps. Since he was in kindergarten, Mr. and Mrs. L. had pushed their son relentlessly to excel in school.

Michael worked hard to be in the top 1 percent of his class. Otherwise, he'd probably never get into Princeton. He worried constantly about his grades.

The worry took its toll. Often a rash broke out on Michael's hands when midterms or finals rolled around. Michael said he always felt as if he lived in a pressure cooker.

In the winter of his junior year, Michael's parents enrolled him in a special course designed to boost Scholastic Aptitude Test (SAT) scores. Michael's scores on the practice test (PSAT) were excellent, but indicated that his SAT score might not be high enough to guarantee admission to Princeton.

The SAT course met three evenings a week, from seven to ten. It also took a lot of study time. But

Academic pressures can be tough. Some students unable to cope with such pressures have attempted suicide.

Michael needed that time for homework. Less time spent on homework meant a drop in class rank.

He began falling behind, even though he studied until one or two in the morning. Exhausted, frazzled, and pressured, he began thinking about jumping off an embankment near his home.

When Michael's quarterly grades came out, indicating a possible drop in class rank, he took the plunge. He thought the drop of several hundred feet would kill him instantly. Then he would be free from the horrible pressure of disappointing his parents.

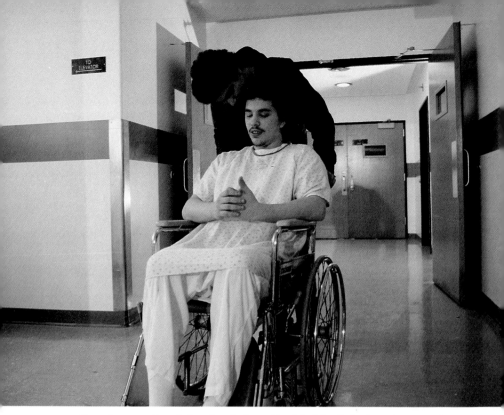

People are often left crippled or disabled by injuries that result from suicide attempts.

But the leap didn't kill Michael. Instead, it severed his spinal cord at the neck. Michael L. is now a quadriplegic, paralyzed from the neck down. For the rest of his life, he will be confined to a wheelchair.

Michael's failed attempt was not unusual. In fact, most teen suicide attempts fail. While many youngsters escape crippling lifetime injuries after a suicide attempt, many others are not so fortunate.

And the results are tragic. In addition to causing lifelong paralysis, suicide attempts have resulted in blindness, loss of limbs, and permanent disfigurement of the face and other parts of the body.

Why are there so many failed suicide attempts? Perhaps the main reason is that a suicide attempt is usually a cry for help, rather than a real effort to kill oneself. *Teens almost never really want to kill themselves.* Most of the time there's a voice inside them that says, "Don't do it!"

And so, fortunately, they don't do the job very well. Unfortunately, however, many do it well enough to sustain lifelong injury.

The fantasies, then, are these:

> *Suicide is a way to get even, and a way to escape an intolerable problem.*

The realities are quite different:

> *Dead people never know whether they got even.*

> *Moreover, if a person fails at a suicide attempt (and most do because they don't really want to die), there's a good chance that another, and possibly worse, problem—disfigurement, paralysis, or some other terrible, permanent injury—will result.*

Any way you look at it, the price is too high for what you get.

A severely depressed person cannot enjoy friendships.

CHAPTER 6

Tunnel Vision

Serious personal problems can make time appear to move in slow motion, so slow that it hardly seems to move at all. Those problems also can block out everything else, including how friends, parents, brothers, and sisters might react to a loved one's death. Nothing seems to matter except the terrible feelings of the moment.

It seems as if the pain will just go on . . . and on . . . and on.

That's the way Lisa P., now nineteen, saw her life a year and a half ago. Lisa suffered from severe depression, a mental state that has been described as an all-encompassing cloud of sadness that follows the depressed person everywhere he or she goes. Listen to Lisa's story on the following pages.

"I had this huge, huge sad feeling inside. I couldn't concentrate and my grades started slipping badly. I found myself in a deep rut and I didn't know how to get out.

"But I was real good at putting on a mask. Nobody suspected how bad I felt. I would just paste on that big smile, and nobody would know.

"Lots of times I wanted to go to my parents and say, 'I need help. I'm in a bad way. I feel like I'm drowning.' But I couldn't do it. Somehow I just couldn't see myself telling them that I needed a shrink.

"So things just kept getting worse and worse. At first I'd have some good days, but near the end I didn't even have any good minutes—or any good seconds! I felt so terrible. So terrible.

"And yet, I was able to keep the mask on. Nobody had the slightest hint of what was going on inside me.

"After a while I started thinking that the only way to end it was to just slit my wrists. I just kept thinking about lying down in a tub and just drifting away.

"But I did it when I knew my mother would find me. I didn't want to die, but at the same time I knew I had to end the pain. It was just too much for me.

"So my mother did find me, and rushed me to the hospital. After I got out, she put me into therapy; I saw a psychiatrist twice a week for about six months.

"All the time I was seeing the psychiatrist, I kept saying to myself, 'This guy isn't helping me at all.' He said it would take time, but I just wasn't seeing any improvement. The pain wasn't going away. He was very cold and distant, and it seemed like he really didn't care about me. Not really.

"So after six months, I tried again. The second time I took sleeping pills. But my mom found me that time, too, and she sent me to another psychiatrist.

"But it was the same thing. This psychiatrist was a woman, so they thought she would be able to relate to me better. She didn't, though.

"So I tried a third time. Pills again. I was really serious about it this time. I didn't want my mom to find me, so I went to a forest preserve on a Saturday afternoon in the winter, when I thought no one would be around.

"But, can you believe it, they were getting ready for a maple syrup festival. These guys were going around putting taps in the trees, and they found me.

"After that, they put me in a psych ward. And that was the best thing that ever happened to me. Because finally—finally!—I found a psychiatrist who knew how to help me!

"For more than a year, nothing changed for me. Then, after four and half months working with the new psychiatrist, the cloud started lifting. The sadness inside just started to evaporate.

"The thing is, if you had told me a year ago that I would be able to be happy again, I wouldn't have believed it."

Today, Lisa is back in school. She's happy with her life, and this time it's not a mask. It's real.

For almost two years, things didn't change for Lisa.

Persons who end their lives give up all chance of recovering—of emerging from their tunnel of depression into the sunlight.

For almost two years, she felt she had nothing to look forward to but unending pain. She tried three times to end it. To Lisa, life just wasn't worth living—then. Now, however, the story is different.

"Every day I thank God for not letting me kill myself. I love living now.

"I guess if there's a lesson to all of it, it's that things *can* change, even though at the time you can't imagine that they will.

"I mean, look at me. I went through two shrinks who didn't do me any good at all. I was so sure that I was at a dead end, and there wasn't any way out. But there was."

When Lisa attempted suicide, she was looking at her life with tunnel vision. The tunnel was heading straight down, into pitch black.

Sometimes people find themselves in tunnels—a period when nothing seems to go right. And those tunnels can be frightening, and deep, and very dark. But no life is an endless tunnel.

And sometimes those who try to help us out of the tunnel, such as Lisa's first two psychiatrists, aren't up to the task. But if a person ends his or her life—dies in the tunnel—he or she will never have a chance to emerge into the sunlight.

Some mental health professionals may be able to help teens overcome depression; others may not.

And there *is* sunlight, as Lisa discovered. Because a person's life never stands still. It changes, and it moves in different directions.

As one young person who attempted suicide, and was later glad the attempt was unsuccessful, stated, "If you choose to live now, you can choose to die later. But if you choose to die now, you can't choose to live later. It just doesn't work that way."

Parents of teens who have committed suicide or attempted suicide are often overcome with guilt. They ask themselves what they've done wrong.

CHAPTER 7

The Family Left Behind

Teens who attempt suicide usually have another kind of tunnel vision. They almost never think about what their death will *really* mean to the people around them. Oh yes, they may fantasize about anguished parents, or a tormented girlfriend or boyfriend with whom they've just broken up. But what they don't realize is that their death could have terrible consequences, far beyond what they imagine.

For openers, their suicide may trigger the death of other people, including their friends (we'll discuss how that can happen in Chapter 8).

In addition, their death undoubtedly will stay with their parents, brothers, and sisters until the day they die. It will place a cloud over the remainder of their lives. For them, nothing will ever be quite the same.

Nobody knows that better than Fred and Trina Westin and their two children, ten-year-old Mark and his twin sister, Debbie. Two years ago, their son and brother, Joey, killed himself.

Mr. and Mrs. Westin agreed to tell their story as long as their real names are not used. Fred, in his early forties, speaks first.

"It's been two years since Joey's death, but it's still hard for me to talk about it. We didn't have any idea what was coming. That morning I took Joey to school, like I always did. He was in the ninth grade, the last year of junior high. I remember that on the way to school we talked about the classes he was going to take in high school the next year. Joey was going to take geometry, biology, English, history, and speech. Something else, but I can't remember.

"We talked about his trying out for the tennis team. He said he wanted to go to a private tennis camp during the summer so he'd have a better chance to make the team. But I said it was too expensive and he should get a part-time job instead. He was a very good player. I didn't think he'd have any problems getting on the junior varsity team. Sophomores never make the varsity team, anyway.

"We started arguing about it. But I was very insistent. I replay that argument over and over. He seemed so upset, but it didn't make any sense. I just keep on trying to figure out if I had handled it differently whether . . ."

Mr. Westin's voice trails off. He pauses, composes himself, then continues.

"Anyway, I dropped him off and went on to work. I don't remember anything that went on at the office that day. All I remember is that at about four in the afternoon I got a frantic call from Trina. She was crying and gasping, and I couldn't understand what she was saying. Finally, I was able to make out that she was at the emergency room at the hospital. Then Marsha, our next-door neighbor, got on the phone and said that Joey had shot himself, and that I should get down to the emergency room right away.

"The rest is kind of like a bad dream—you know, how you just have this horrible feeling in your gut. Everything just kind of moves in slow motion. Everything seems distorted.

"When I got to the emergency room, Marsha was there, but I didn't see Trina or the twins.

Joey was rushed to the emergency room soon after he shot himself.

I was trying to remain calm, but inside I was very panicky. I had this panicky, gnawing feeling of impending doom. I can't really describe it . . . just a terrible feeling that everything was all wrong—like you're drowning and you can't save yourself.

"Marsha told me that Trina was inside with some doctors and that she had dropped off the twins at my sister's house. A nurse led me inside, where they take the emergency cases, and I saw Trina sitting outside the door of one of the rooms there. She looked tiny and helpless, like a rag doll. She was just slumping in the chair. As soon as she saw me, she broke down. I wanted to ask her

As soon as Mr. Westin saw the look on the doctor's face, he knew Joey had died.

what happened, but I couldn't. She wouldn't have been able to answer me, anyway. She was kind of beside herself. I just tried to comfort her, telling her that it would be all right.

"After a few minutes, a doctor came out of the room. As soon as I looked at him—saw the look on his face—I knew Joey hadn't made it. Trina knew, too. She opened her mouth, and . . ."

Fred stops again to compose himself. He puts his head in his hands, pauses for perhaps thirty seconds, then continues.

"She opened her mouth . . . and . . . and out came this terrible wailing moan. I'll never forget that sound. It was so horrible, like all the pain of the world wrapped up in one sound.

"Our pastor came in and we drove back to the house. He stayed with us, and then some people from our church came with dinner. I don't remember too much about that evening except that I was just totally numb. The only thing I do remember, something that will live with me until the day I die, is that some women from the church came in and cleaned the bedroom. I saw them going in with buckets and mops. And I thought, 'They're going in there to clean parts of my son off the wall.'

"The next several days were impossible. I didn't sleep at all. Finally I just collapsed. When I woke up, I tried to convince myself that I had just had a very bad dream. But immediately, that feeling that something very wrong had happened came back.

"After two years, things are kind of back to normal. But naturally, they'll never really be completely normal again. Not really.

"At night, Trina and I still lie awake and try to figure out how it could have happened. We talk about things we should or shouldn't have done. I know it's useless. But we can't help ourselves."

Trina Westin is active in a support group that helps relatives of suicide victims work through their grief and trauma. Although she has given many speeches to church and community groups about her loss, she still becomes emotional when talking about Joey.

"The biggest thing is that there is a hole left in your life that will never be filled. It's an emptiness that never goes away.

"Joey and I were always very close. And I think that has been the hardest thing for me to deal with—the fact that I always thought that I could sense his moods, and could talk to him when things weren't going right for him.

"That day, he came home from school in a pretty rotten mood. He said that Fred had told him that he couldn't go to tennis camp, and he couldn't understand why.

Some youngsters may need special help when a brother or sister has committed suicide. Members of the clergy are often trained to do this special counseling.

"I told him that it was very expensive—that his father and I had talked it over, and we didn't feel that it was necessary. For some reason, he just didn't want to accept that, which was very unusual for him because normally he was a very level-headed kid. If you gave him a logical reason for a decision, he would accept it.

"I asked him how school was, but he wouldn't answer like he normally did. He just mumbled something and went to his room. I just had no idea how upset he was.

"I went about cooking dinner. The twins had come home from their piano lesson and began doing their chores. They fed the dog and began setting the dinner table. After about fifteen minutes, I heard a loud *pop!* The dog was still eating, and his head jerked up from his bowl.

"For a fraction of a second, time seemed to stand still. I looked over at the twins and they were just standing there at the kitchen table, stiff and erect, their eyes open wide.

"'Joey,' I yelled. 'What was that?' There wasn't any response. 'Joey, are you all right?'

"Then, all of a sudden, the strangest feeling came over me. I can't explain it. It was like I suddenly became icy cold. I shuddered all over.

"I ran to Joey's room but he wasn't there. Our room is just down the hall. I ran out of

Joey's room, and then I saw him on our bedroom floor. Well, I couldn't really see all of him. I just saw his hand from behind our bed and our .22 Magnum lying next to it. I went into complete shock.

"By this time the twins had come down the hall. They were screaming, 'Mommy, what's wrong? Where's Joey?' I honestly don't remember what happened at that point, but I think I told them to run and get Marsha.

"Marsha must have had the presence of mind to call for an ambulance, because by the time she came over I could hear the sirens. The firehouse is only a couple of blocks away. I do remember seeing the paramedics rushing in with all their equipment. By that time, I was cradling Joey in my arms. I can't describe how he looked; you'll have to forgive me. It was the worst nightmare imaginable.

"The strangest thing about it was that I felt like I was watching myself, and that none of it was real. A part of me was outside my body, up on the ceiling, and I could see myself holding Joey and I could hear myself

Brothers and sisters of teens who commit suicide may think that they were responsible for the teenager's act.

crying uncontrollably. But the pain, the anguish, kept on pulling me back inside myself.

"There will always be parts of that experience that will haunt me. Holding Joey is one of them, and his funeral is another one.

"Then there's the feeling that if I had done something differently, maybe Joey would still be alive today. All of us have gone through therapy—we've been to family counseling for two years, now—to help us get through this. I understand that it's not good to second-guess yourself, but it's awfully hard not to.

"Joey's death has been very hard on the twins. At first they had nightmares about the experience several times a week. Even now, once in a while, they still have them.

"They idolized Joey. He was a hero to them. He helped them with their schoolwork and spent time playing with them. They thought that they had done something wrong—that somehow they were responsible for what happened. For several months, every so often, they'd ask if Joey had done it because he was mad at them.

"Mark, who was always a very good student, began having a lot of problems in school. He was very hyper and couldn't concentrate. We had to take him to a psychiatrist, in addition to going to the family counselor.

"And then, it was just devastating to my mother. Joey was her first grandchild, and I think she had a special place in her heart for him. After the funeral, she was just never the same. She became very depressed. She was a very outgoing person, but afterward she never went out much. We tried to get her out, but it was hard because we were really trying to put the pieces back together for ourselves. She died seven months after Joey. I'm not saying his suicide killed her because she was pretty sick, anyway. But I think she died sooner than she would have. After Joey's death, I believe she just lost the will to live.

"Sometimes I get very angry at Joey. 'Why did you have to put us through this?' I ask. He was such a good kid. He never gave us any trouble. At this point, I have very fond memories of him. He had such a great sense of humor, and he was so warm and loving. But sometimes, I can't help but feel some bitterness toward him."

Joey Westin was a pleasant youngster. He was not, by any stretch of the imagination, mean or cruel. Had he truly understood what his suicide would mean to his family, it could be that he *never* would have shot himself.

But now, of course, it's too late.

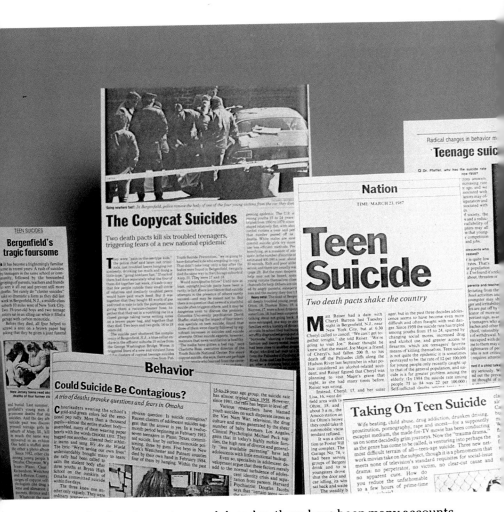

During the past several decades, there have been many accounts of cluster suicides in the press.

CHAPTER 8

Cluster Suicides

Youngsters who commit suicide have tunnel vision in another respect. They don't understand that their suicide can trigger *other* teen suicides. So in a sense, they may be responsible not only for their own destruction, but for the deaths of others as well.

Cluster suicides are incidents in which one suicide encourages others. During the past several decades, there have been many accounts of these tragedies in the news media. And they have occurred in every part of the country.

One of the most publicized in recent years occurred in Bergenfield, New Jersey, a suburban community near New York City. The first to die there was Joseph Major, a high school dropout who fell from a cliff after drinking heavily. Some thought Joseph's death was accidental, but four of his friends weren't so sure.

Thomas Olton, Thomas Rizzo, Cheryl Burress, and her sister, Lisa, brooded over Joseph's death. They visited his grave and wept openly. Finally, they decided to end their lives, too. They filled Thomas Olton's Camaro with gas, drove to an apartment complex, pulled the car into a garage there, closed the door, and left the motor running. The lifeless bodies of all four were found the next morning.

But the tragedy didn't end there. Some seven hundred miles to the west, in Alsip, Illinois, Karen Logan and her best friend, Nancy Grannan, read about the terrible events in Bergenfield. Both girls had serious personal problems, and decided to kill themselves in a manner similar to the deaths of the foursome in New Jersey.

Three years earlier, a cluster of teen suicides claimed six young lives in Clear Lake City, Texas, near the Johnson Space Center. And the following year, an outbreak of "copycat" suicides hit Plano, Texas, a suburb of Dallas.

The experts suspect there are several factors at work in cluster suicides. One of them may be misguided loyalty.

Dr. Mary Giffin, a noted authority on teen suicide, has described how misguided loyalty works. Dr. Giffin believes that when a teen kills himself, some of his friends may begin to sympathize with his problems. They may say to themselves, "Nobody really knew Mack like I did. He was such a great guy. Sure, he had

Press reports of a suicide may incite a troubled youngster to kill himself or herself.

problems. Just like me. Just like everybody else. Mack was too good for all the garbage that was heaped on him. No one gave him a chance."

Then they may think, "Everybody says that Mack was crazy. But he *wasn't*." (In this respect, the friends are probably right. Very few people who attempt suicide are insane. They're merely unaware that there are ways, other than suicide, to solve their problems.)

Teachers and other adults who say suicide is "crazy" may make the victim's friends angry and resentful.

Finally, they may begin to feel that they "owe it to their friend to join him in death." These feelings of loyalty may be particularly strong if parents, teachers, and classmates say the suicide was "crazy," or don't seem to feel the loss as passionately as the victim's friends.

72

Loyalty is a noble attribute. But when a friend takes his own life, "joining him in death" is not an act of loyalty. It is repeating a tragic mistake.

Not all cluster suicides result from misguided loyalty, of course. Others may take place after stories of a suicide appear in the media. Experts say some youngsters may have been thinking about suicide, and then are "pushed over the edge" by such news stories, especially those that glamorize or trivialize the victim's death. (See Chapter 4.)

A large body of research seems to support that view. For instance, statistics gathered by sociologist David Phillips, a leading authority on suicide, suggest that suicide rates may have jumped as much as 31 percent in Los Angeles three days after a suicide was reported in the *Los Angeles Times*. Dr. Phillips came up with similar results in Detroit. He also found that suicide rates jumped throughout the country when a suicide was reported in the national media.

Those jumps may be particularly noticeable when the suicide victim is a celebrity. The teen suicide rate went up for several weeks after actor Freddie Prinze, a popular television star in the 1970s, took his life.

Seeing their lives only with tunnel vision, then, people who kill themselves may unknowingly push other victims—friends and acquaintances—toward their graves. People who kill themselves may also do serious emotional harm to the people they love—brothers, sisters, and parents.

Most teens would enjoy going to camp. Depressed teens, however, probably wouldn't. Nor would they take pleasure in friendships, hobbies, or anything else.

CHAPTER 9

Depression and
Teen Suicide

If teens who attempt suicide don't think about the disastrous effect their death will have on family and friends, then what *are* they thinking?

According to the experts, more than 80 percent of the time they are extremely depressed, and so their minds are focused on the terrible emotional pain in which they find themselves. In their depression, they often dwell on what they feel is their unlucky and helpless lot in life. And they think that their situation is hopeless.

Depressed individuals usually don't understand that, in all likelihood, their plight really *isn't* hopeless. Situations that appear totally bleak often don't turn out as bad as imagined.

Also, everyone is unlucky at times. But depressed persons usually aren't able to grasp that, either.

And the only people who are genuinely helpless are those who are profoundly retarded, or those who suffer from physical disabilities that completely restrict their movement.

But again, deeply depressed persons do not—often *cannot*—understand that their feelings of having no luck, and of being helpless and hopeless, do not reflect reality.

Nevertheless, their feelings are very real. And as we'll discuss later, they should never be dismissed as "crazy." In fact, the feelings may be completely understandable in light of what has happened to the suicidal person. Think back to Michelle C., in Chapter 5.

Feelings of depression are real—and often understandable.

Michelle's depression was certainly understandable considering her abusive, alcoholic father. Or consider Michael L., also in Chapter 5. If you recall, Michael was constantly under pressure to produce high grades so that he would be admitted to his parents' alma mater. Michael's depression was understandable, too, considering his stressful situation.

Besides feeling pressured and abused, some teens who suffer from depression may feel isolated—set far apart from their classmates and family. They may feel that they simply have no one to talk to, no one with whom they can share their thoughts, dreams, and fears. Young people whose parents, through job transfers, move their children from one city to another are more likely than others to feel extreme loneliness and isolation. And such feelings can lead to depression.

Still others may feel that they, as individuals, have no value, and never will. Parents who call their child worthless or stupid, or who physically abuse the youngster, often spark depression.

Bill D. is an example. Bill's mother, a woman with a severe emotional problem, liked to call her son "garbage-brain." Whenever Bill did anything that displeased her, she hit him—sometimes with her hands, sometimes with a belt, sometimes with an iron. She constantly told him that he would never amount to anything. When he won the school spelling bee in the sixth grade, she accused him of cheating. (He didn't.)

When Bill entered high school at 14, an alert school psychologist noticed that his behavior indicated depression. After many discussions with Bill, the psychologist's suspicions were confirmed. Along the way, he determined that Mrs. D.'s cruel treatment of her son led to the depression.

While most teen depression results from events in the youngster's life, it occasionally occurs when there's a chemical imbalance in the brain. When a chemical imbalance is present, the depression usually can be treated with medicines.

Some depressed teens become angry and defiant.

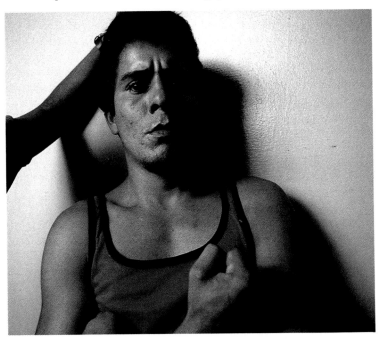

Regardless of the cause, depressed teens usually don't act normally. In some cases, they may take no pleasure in friendships, schoolwork, hobbies, or anything else. They may sleep a great deal. They seem to have no interests. Using almost all of their energy to focus on their sadness, they have no energy left for anything else. (Remember, depressed persons have not brought on their condition intentionally. Without expert counseling, and sometimes medicine, they can't just "turn off" their depression. Telling them to "snap out of it" will do no good.)

Although some depressed teens become listless, it's more likely that they'll become angry, defiant, and sometimes reckless. They may turn to drugs and alcohol. They may steal, cut classes, set fires, fight with other youngsters, or run away from home.

Much of this behavior is self-destructive, a kind of slow suicide. Instead of using a gun or a rope, these victims may kill themselves slowly, over a period of several years.

Laura L., now sixteen, is an example of a depressed teen who attempted to commit slow suicide. As you read her story, keep in mind that throughout her entire ordeal, no one—including Laura herself—recognized that she suffered from depression.

The daughter of two schoolteachers, Laura began smoking marijuana when she was thirteen. By the time she reached high school, she was also a heavy alcohol abuser, and was beginning to use cocaine.

Laura began smoking marijuana at age thirteen, when her brother and his best friend gave her a "joint."

Laura never got good grades. As a freshman, she decided that the best way to find friends was to socialize with the "burnouts" and "losers" who congregated outside her school. She thought that their acceptance would make her feel better. But it didn't.

Laura's depression deepened. And as it did, she became more defiant. She talked back to her teachers, cut classes, and refused to do her class work. After she got into a serious fight, she was expelled.

She ran away from home after being expelled, and lived at a friend's house. Her friend's mother gave Laura drugs and alcohol. For a time, the drugs and alcohol masked her sadness. But to get money for more, Laura stole from department stores—mostly clothing that she sold to friends. She was caught, put on probation, and sent home to her parents. She ran away again.

After a serious fight, the principal at Laura's school expelled her.

By now it was clear to everyone, Laura included, that something was seriously wrong. But what? No one was able to get a handle on Laura's problem.

One night, after she had tried to drown her dreadful sadness in a bottle of whiskey, she discovered that the alcohol had no effect.

So Laura, seeking to escape her never-ending anguish, took her mother's car onto a nearby expressway and pushed the accelerator pedal to the floor. She approached a tollway booth at approximately ninety-five miles per hour. But she didn't slow down. Laura aimed the car at a cement divider that separated the tollbooths.

Three weeks later, she awoke from a coma. She found herself in a hospital room, a mass of broken bones and ruptured organs.

One day later, she began an eight-month program

Drug abusers often steal to support their habit. Such actions help destroy their self-esteem.

of physical—and mental—rehabilitation. Again, until she wound up in the hospital, no one had realized that Laura suffered from depression. She was just labeled a "rebellious, defiant, nasty kid." A staff psychiatrist who had seen similar cases suspected Laura's depression and began treating her.

Today, Laura is a different person. She's back in school and making good grades. In addition, she's planning to go to college so that she can become a psychiatric social worker.

Laura's story illustrates several important points. The first is that depression is often overlooked when parents, teachers, and school officials try to find the reasons for defiant, angry behavior.

The second point is that drugs and depression often go hand in hand. And it's not always clear which came first. One thing is *perfectly* clear, however: Drug

Some drugs take the edge off depression for a while. Eventually, however, they make the depression worse.

abuse often causes the depression to deepen. Although some drugs, such as cocaine, can make a depressed person feel better for a while, they eventually change the brain's chemistry so that feeling pleasure becomes impossible.

And a person who cannot feel pleasure is a person who is depressed.

Finally, drugs can deepen depression by causing people to behave in ways that destroy their self-esteem (which is undoubtedly very low in the first place). Drug abusers often steal, cheat, and lie to support their habit.

Drugs, then, can grease the skids to suicide. They help suck depressed people into a whirlpool of self-destruction. Around and around, faster and faster they spin, downward into their chemical dependence—downward toward the black hole at the center.

Teens who are planning suicide often tell their friends.

CHAPTER 10

When a Friend Contemplates Suicide

Let's suppose that you're walking home after school with your best friend, whom we'll call Kirk. Usually Kirk is talkative and cheerful. But during the past month—and this week, especially—he's been very sullen and withdrawn.

Kirk sits next to you in your math and social studies classes, and you've noticed that he's failed several exams in the past few weeks. That's very unusual for Kirk, who is normally a solid B student.

After you've walked a few blocks, Kirk suddenly turns to you and says glumly, "I want to give you my tape collection."

You look at him in disbelief. Kirk's tapes are his most prized possession. He's spent years collecting them. "What?" you ask. "You've got to be kidding!"

"No, I'm serious," he replies. "I've listened to them

a thousand times, and I'm sick of them." Kirk looks at you with a hollow stare. He looks tired and pale. It's obvious that he hasn't had a lot of sleep lately.

A scene similar to the one we've just described should put you on notice: Kirk could be thinking about killing himself.

Your friend has just displayed several of the danger signs psychologists say point to a potential suicide attempt.

First, Kirk says he wants to give away his tape collection. Experts say that giving away personal possessions may mean that the person is "getting his or her affairs in order" before trying to commit suicide.

Another sign is the change in Kirk's mood. Becoming passive or sullen is another indication of serious trouble.

Kirk's obvious lack of sleep is still another warning sign. People who contemplate suicide often experience a change in sleeping habits, and generally have difficulty sleeping.

Finally, the drop in Kirk's grades suggests a problem.

Other signs of an impending suicide attempt include the following:

- Angry, hostile behavior
- Alcohol and/or drug abuse

- A change in eating habits, often a lack of interest in food

- Losing interest in school, friends, hobbies

- A deep fear of leaving home

- A sudden change in personality (for example, from being an easygoing person to becoming an aggressive, overbearing, or obnoxious individual)

- Impulsive behavior (doing things suddenly without any logical reason)

- Sudden, wide swings in mood (being deeply depressed one day, joyous the next, or vice versa)

- Loss of friends, or not being able to make friends

- An inability to concentrate

- Saying that everything is hopeless

- Talking about death all the time

- Becoming sexually promiscuous (As a way to relieve depression, sleeping around doesn't work any better than drugs and alcohol. Usually, it only deepens the depression.)

- Making out a will

Alcohol and drug abuse may be a sign of an upcoming suicide attempt.

As you may have noticed, many of these signs are the same as those mentioned for depression.

Now, let's suppose that you're aware of the warning signs, and so recognize that Kirk may be contemplating suicide. What should you say to him?

You might say, "I've been worried about you, Kirk. You seem like you've got a lot on your mind lately. Want to talk about it?"

If Kirk says yes and then begins to tell you about his depression, or how he thinks something—or everything—is going wrong in his life, that's a good start.

If he says no, you shouldn't drop the subject. Remember, Kirk has displayed four danger signs. Something is probably wrong—perhaps seriously wrong—and you're his friend. Friends are supposed to help each other when things get tough.

Even if Kirk turns aggressive or hostile, saying something like "Leave me alone," or "I don't want to talk about it," or "It's none of your business," or "It hasn't got anything to do with you," you still shouldn't drop the subject. Friends are there to help—even when it's not easy.

So you might say something like, "No, I won't leave you alone. You're my best friend. It's clear that you've got a big problem, and I want to help you. That's what friends are for. Tell me what's up, Kirk."

At that point, Kirk will probably open up. Once he understands that you're truly interested in his problems—and that you're not going to leave him alone until he talks to you—he'll want to get everything off his chest.

Once Kirk starts opening up, it's your job to listen sympathetically. That means really listen. Kirk may be contemplating suicide because, at least in part, he thinks that no one will understand how he feels. You can help dispel those dangerous feelings by being a good listener.

So whatever you do, don't tell Kirk that he "shouldn't feel that way"—or that his feelings are "stupid" or "crazy."

A good listener takes a troubled person's problems seriously and shows interest and concern for feelings of depression.

His feelings are not stupid or crazy. Feelings are a natural response to things that happen to us. And without professional counseling, most depressed people can't help how they feel.

As Kirk discusses his problems, he may say that he's been thinking about killing himself. He might come right out and say it, or he may mention it indirectly by saying something like "The world would be better without me," or "You won't have to worry about me much longer."

If he does, you should not tell him how "dumb" or "crazy" suicide is. Kirk doesn't want to hear that. He wants a sympathetic ear. At this point, your job as a friend isn't to judge Kirk's response to his problems. It's to prevent him from killing himself by listening and by finding out his plans about suicide.

If Kirk doesn't mention suicide, you should bring up the subject. Don't be afraid that you'll put ideas into Kirk's head. If he is considering suicide, the idea is already there; if he's not, your mentioning it isn't going to convince him to do it. It just doesn't work that way.

You could say, "I can see why you feel so depressed about everything that's been dumped on you. When things get bad like that, it's normal to feel like ending it all. So, have you thought about it?"

Let's suppose that Kirk says yes. At that point, you should find out if he's made plans. You might ask something like, "Have you planned how you're going to do it?"

But whatever you do, don't say anything like, "Oh, you don't really feel like killing yourself." (He probably does.) Don't say, "You'll get over it. Things will be better tomorrow." (They might not be.) And don't say, "You'd never really do that." (Yes, he might.)

In short, don't criticize, judge, ridicule, or minimize Kirk's feelings. That could only anger and depress him more. But do accept his feelings, and show your real interest and concern.

If Kirk has made specific plans to kill himself, then you must not leave him until you can get a responsible adult to be with him. Kirk must not be left alone. Call his parents, your parents, a teacher or school counselor you trust, your clergyman, a teen-center worker, a counselor at a suicide-prevention center (see Chapter 11), or any other responsible adult who

Any drugs or chemicals that could be used to kill oneself should be removed from the house.

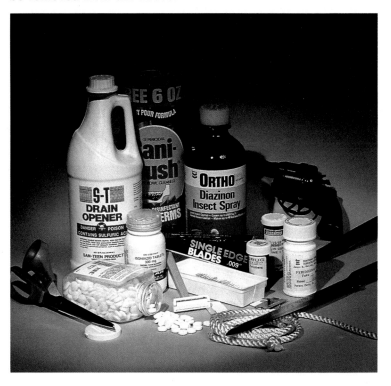

can help. Tell that person immediately that Kirk may be seriously thinking about committing suicide, and that you will stay with Kirk until the adult arrives.

Make certain that the adult understands that everything that Kirk could possibly use to kill himself—ropes, medicines, razor blades, household cleaners, guns, poisons, and sleeping pills—must be promptly removed from his house.

Even if Kirk hasn't made any specific plans, you still must contact his parents or another responsible adult as soon as possible.

Don't make the mistake of thinking that after you and your friend hash things out, he or she will get better. A person who seriously thinks about committing suicide needs professional counseling. You may be able to perform an invaluable service by being a good listener. But only a trained professional can resolve the underlying causes of your friend's anguish.

And now, one final—but very important—point: Teens who discuss their planned suicides often swear their friends to secrecy. If that ever happens to you, you must betray the trust, and tell a responsible adult. Think how you would feel if you remained silent, and your friend killed himself or herself. For the rest of your life, you would have to live with the terrible knowledge that you might have saved your friend's life—but didn't.

The choice is easy when you have to pick between a dead friend or a broken promise.

Counselors at crisis intervention centers are trained to help suicidal teens through tough times.

CHAPTER 11

Other Ways

Suicidal teens generally are not able to grasp that killing oneself is the *least desirable* way to relieve their sadness and pain. As we've already stated, they think suicide is the *only way.*

But of course, there are other ways.

In a time of crisis—when a youngster is on the verge of taking his or her life, or has actually made an attempt—the most important order of business is to make certain that he or she survives. Then, afterward, the alternatives to suicide can be explored.

A suicide-prevention center is designed to save lives and to help people find other ways to relieve their suffering. There are several hundred of these agencies located throughout the United States. And almost all of them have trained volunteers who answer emergency phone calls twenty-four hours a day, seven days a week.

The phone counselors at the centers know how to talk to suicidal teens. They can keep a troubled youngster on the phone until the urge to kill himself or herself passes. (Studies show that suicidal urges last only a short time.)

Personnel at suicide-prevention centers also know how to quickly contact paramedics and ambulance services if a suicide attempt has been made. If callers won't give an address, the volunteers keep them on the line until the call can be traced.

A person can reach the nearest suicide-prevention center by dialing 411, 0, or 911. The number also can be found in the Yellow Pages by looking under "Suicide," "Crisis," "Mental Health," or "Counseling."

In addition to suicide-prevention centers, there are two other organizations, Contact and The Samaritans, that have been established to help people who are contemplating suicide. If those organizations are in your community, their telephone numbers can be found in the white pages.

Each suicide-prevention counselor has a list of mental health agencies and professionals who know how to help young people deal with their problems. Once the immediate crisis has passed, the counselors usually refer troubled adolescents to those institutions or persons.

Often, they suggest local mental health clinics that are supported by the government. These institutions usually have at least one psychiatrist as well as psy-

A suicide-prevention center may be found in the Yellow Pages under "Suicide Prevention Service," "Suicide," "Crisis," "Mental Health," or "Social Services."

chologists, social workers, counselors, and other mental health professionals.

In the best of all possible worlds, every mental health professional would quickly and efficiently assist every person who seeks help. Unfortunately, that's not always the case. As with Lisa P., whom you met in Chapter 6, a suicidal teen may not be lucky the first (or even the second or third) time around.

Different mental health professionals take different approaches, and not every approach works for every

Some teens must see several counselors before finding one who can help.

patient. And, unfortunately, there are also some psychiatrists, psychologists, social workers, and counselors who are not very good at what they do. So people who feel they aren't getting better after a reasonable amount of time should try elsewhere.

If a person persists, there's a good chance that he or she eventually will find someone who can help. Finding the right counselor can be very difficult, it can take time, but it can be done. And the results are always worth the effort.

Besides personnel at mental health centers, school counselors and members of the clergy can suggest professionals who might help. Family doctors usually are able to make suggestions, also.

Learning how to cope with life's difficulties may take only a few months' work with a psychiatrist or psychologist. Or it may take many years. "Many years" may seem like a terribly long time to most patients. But when it's over, they almost always say they're glad they stuck with it.

When working with teens, most psychiatrists and psychologists use what's called "talking therapy." Through conversation, they help their young patients understand the true nature of their problems (which, without the help of a professional, may be next to impossible to determine). Then they help the youngster find realistic ways to solve the problem. Or, if the problem can't be solved, they help find ways to cope with it.

Sometimes psychiatrists, who are medical doctors, may prescribe medicine to help the patient. But they frequently don't use medicine when treating teens.

There was a time when people felt ashamed if they needed a psychologist or psychiatrist. There was a time when people believed they should be able to solve their problems without professional help.

Fortunately, those days are gone. Informed, intelligent people understand that some problems are too complex and too deep for any individual to handle by himself or herself. Thinking about killing oneself is an example of such a problem.

When a teen is serious about suicide, it's time for professional help.

Suicidal teens often make out a will or give away their
possessions.

C H A P T E R 12

Frequently Asked Questions About Teen Suicide

How serious is the problem of teen suicide?

Very serious. Each year, more than five thousand young people kill themselves. In a major study of high school students recently completed, one out of every five teens reported severe problems with self-esteem, and thoughts of suicide. Officially, suicide is the third leading cause of death among people fifteen to twenty-four years old in the United States. But most experts believe that it's really the second leading cause of death, since many suicides are erroneously listed as accidents.

Why do so many teenagers kill themselves?

There's no single cause. But many experts believe that the deterioration of the family unit, rootlessness in American society, excessive television viewing, a breakdown in religious and moral values, and drug and alcohol abuse are important factors. There are undoubtedly many more.

What precipitates a suicide attempt?

First, there is an underlying mental state, usually depression. Most people are depressed from time to time, but the depression lifts. Suicidal persons often suffer from extreme and prolonged depression. A "trigger event" may occur when the person is depressed, and that may precipitate a suicide attempt.

What's a "trigger event"?

Usually the loss of something or someone very important to the teen. A parent may leave through divorce. A brother or sister may die suddenly. A girlfriend or boyfriend may move away. There are instances of young people who have become so upset after losing a game of "Dungeons and Dragons" that they have killed themselves. Other kinds of losses can be equally traumatic. For example, when a talented high school basketball player was expelled for smoking marijuana on school grounds, he lost the prestige of being a sports star in his school. He also felt that he had lost his chance to receive a sports scholarship at a major university. These losses triggered his suicide attempt.

Does suicide run in families?

There's no scientific evidence of a "suicide gene" that can be inherited. However, when a parent commits suicide, his or her child may believe suicide is an

Scientists have not found any evidence of a "suicide gene" that could be inherited.

acceptable way to resolve problems. For that reason, say some experts, children of suicide victims have a higher suicide rate than other young people.

Aren't most suicides unplanned acts that are done on the spur of the moment?

No. Most suicidal people plan their deaths carefully, sometimes weeks or months in advance.

Aren't people who attempt suicide insane?

While it is true that there are some suicidal people who suffer from profound mental illness, their numbers are relatively few. The overwhelming majority of people who attempt suicide are sane.

Isn't it true that teens who talk about killing themselves never do?

Actually, it's just the opposite. Most suicidal teens who talk about killing themselves are crying out for help. They're saying, "I'm in such terrible pain, I really will kill myself if I'm not helped." And they will. So it's up to any friend or acquaintance who hears a teen talking about committing suicide to intervene—to find a responsible adult who can help.

If a teenager is under a psychiatrist's or psychologist's care, then he or she won't commit suicide, right?

Unfortunately, that's not the case. Some suicidal youngsters may require many months, and sometimes even years, of treatment in order to cope with their problems. During that time, suicide is possible. In fact, some people who suffer from severe depression are more likely to kill themselves soon after the depression begins to lift. When they were severely depressed, they simply didn't have the energy to kill themselves; once the depression begins to lessen, they find that energy.

How can you tell if a friend is thinking about suicide?

Suicidal teens are often angry and hostile. They may abuse drugs and/or alcohol. They may have sudden personality changes or wide swings in mood. They may lose interest in school, friends, and hobbies. Normal eating and sleeping habits may change, also. Suicidal youths may lose their ability to concentrate, and they may dwell on death, make out a will or give away their possessions, become sexually promiscuous, and act impulsively. They may talk about how hopeless everything is. Sometimes suicidal teens show none of these signs, however.

If a person really wants to kill himself or herself, it seems like there's really nothing anyone can do to prevent it.

Not so. There's usually a great deal that can be done. That's because most suicidal youngsters have mixed feelings about killing themselves. On one hand, they desperately want to escape from their terrible sadness and pain; on the other, they really don't want to die. If they can be shown that they can escape from their anguish without killing themselves, they'll opt for life. Sadly, however, there are probably a small number of youngsters who can't be convinced that there are better ways than suicide to deal with their problems. They will find a way to kill themselves regardless of the quality of professional help or loving support from friends and family.

If a friend acts recklessly, is he or she trying to commit suicide?

Recklessness can be a form of suicidal behavior. Perhaps the most common example of suicidal behavior is reckless driving, which tragically can claim not only the life of the suicide victim, but also the lives of innocent individuals who happen to be in the wrong place at the wrong time. Driving while under the influence of drugs and/or alcohol is another common form of reckless behavior. Sometimes, suicidal youths will find creative ways to place themselves in a dangerous situation. One teen took a subway to the most dangerous part of town late at night, got out, and flaunted money in front of thugs. When he was robbed, he taunted the thieves, and was savagely beaten. Before the attack, one of the thieves said, "This guy wants to die."

How does a suicidal person find help?

Talking to a school counselor, a favorite teacher, a clergyman, or teen-center counselor is a good place to start. A family doctor can help, also.

Family counseling can help a troubled teen's parents and brothers and sisters deal with the teen's anger and depression in a positive way.

Many towns and cities have a mental health facility. You can usually find its phone number in the Yellow Pages under "Mental Health," or "Counseling." These institutions almost always have a person who can help suicidal teens.

Most cities and larger towns also have suicide-prevention centers that have twenty-four-hour, seven-day-a-week emergency phone numbers. To reach the center, simply call 411, 0, or 911, or look in the Yellow Pages under "Suicide," "Crisis," "Mental Health," or "Counseling." In some areas, suicide prevention numbers are listed at the front of the phone book.

I N D E X

ABOUT THE AUTHOR

Warren Colman began his career in 1967 as a Washington correspondent for CBS radio. While in Washington, he covered the White House, the Pentagon, and Capitol Hill.

He left CBS to teach in Chicago for three years, after which he joined the educational film division of *Esquire* magazine. As an executive producer there, he was responsible for the output of more than 10 independent production companies. Also in that position, he served as script supervisor for more than 35 productions annually.

After spending almost four years at *Esquire*, Mr. Colman joined SA films, an independent film production company headquartered in New Jersey. As vice-president of SA, Mr. Colman was actively involved in all aspects of production, including budgeting, scripting, location, and talent coordination, direction, and post-production supervision.

After three years at SA, Mr. Colman formed his own company, the Colman Communications Corporation, to specialize in the production of educational media, and provide editorial services for business and industry. For the past 12 years, he has written hundreds of informational and educational films, video presentations, multi-image shows, live industrial theater, filmstrips, and audio programs.

Mr. Colman's editorial services are used by a large number of Fortune 500 companies and leading distributors of educational media. He has produced many works on AIDS information, including a film, *AIDS: What Every Kid Should Know,* distributed by Barr Films, and a filmstrip and videostrip, *Understanding and Preventing AIDS.*

Productions he has written have won more than 40 national and international awards, including the CINE Golden Eagle (American Film Festival); Gold Camera, Silver Screen, and Certificates for Creative Excellence (U.S. Industrial); Gold, Silver, and Bronze Awards (Festival of the Americas/Houston International Film Festival); "Best of the Year" (*Preview* magazine and *Media & Methods* magazine).

Mr. Colman received his BSJ in 1966 and his MSJ in 1967 from Northwestern University Medill School of Journalism. He lives with his wife and three children in Glenview, Illinois.